# Whose Coat is that Jacket Hanging on the Floor?

## Stories of Welsh Mothers and their Lost Children

Lewis Thomas

The stories presented may be considered upsetting or triggering for some readers as it includes incidences of violence, abuse, substance use, trauma, and grief. Due to this mature content, this book is recommended for adult readers.

Permission was given to share these stories and all identifying information, including names, ages, dates, and locations have been changed or removed for confidentiality purposes.

First published 2023
by Rowanvale Books Ltd
The Gate
Keppoch Street
Roath
Cardiff
CF24 3JW
www.rowanvalebooks.com

A CIP catalogue record for this book is available from the British Library.
ISBN: 978-1-914422-16-4
eBook ISBN: 978-1-914422-17-1

Permission was given to share these stories.

All names, dates, locations and other identifying information have been changed or removed for confidentiality purposes.

All proceeds will be donated to charity to support mothers in similar situations.

# Table of Contents

# Whose Coat is that Jacket Hanging on the Floor?

*Lewis Thomas*

During the three years I resided in Wales, I came across a number of Welsh sayings and idioms, but none so frequently as "Whose coat is that jacket hanging on the floor?" There appears to be no known record of when this phrase first appeared, nor much agreement as to what exactly it means. One Welsh woman stated that it was created to confuse foreigners like myself.

I have come to use this phrase as a description of the mothers I have worked with over the past couple of years who have had their children permanently removed from their care. Previous research refers to these women as "maternal outcasts". I believe that the phrase "Whose coat is that jacket hanging on the floor?" best describes their experience. I believe this due to three aspects of this phrase.

Firstly, from the outset it creates a sense of displacement and confusion, as though things don't quite make sense. This state is one that these mothers know and experience all too frequently.

Secondly, there is an object; however, it is unclear as to what specifically it is. Is it a coat, or is it a jacket? Similarly, these mothers are unsure as to what their identity is, especially in relation to their motherhood. They were mothers with children, but are now mothers without children. In this way, their motherhood is ambiguous and contradictory, such that it appears that they are both mothers and not mothers at the same time, much like the conclusion of whether it is a coat, or whether it is a jacket.

Thirdly, this phrase refers to a place, but again it is unclear as to where exactly it is referring to. Is the object hanging up or is it on the floor? Similarly, these mothers' place in society is just as ambiguous and confusing. It is "this in-between state in a society which offers no validation or guidance..." (Memarnia, Nolte, Norris & Harborne, 2015, p. 307). They are often displaced, both physically and socially, outside of certainty and stability, much like the coat-jacket somewhere between hanging and the floor. This experience of uncertainty and instability is not only present currently for these mothers but has often been present in their lives long before they were mothers.

These themes are underlying throughout the stories presented, and it is important for us, as a society, to genuinely reflect on how these women got to be where they are and really question: whose coat is that jacket hanging on the floor?

## Maternal Outcasts and Collateral Consequences

*"Child removal can no longer be seen as the end of the problem." (Broadhurst & Mason, 2017, p. 45)*

The intention of this section is to briefly present a backdrop of research and information associated with mothers who have had children removed from their care. It is also my intention to do this in a way that minimises objectifying or pathologising these mothers but rather seeks to honour and acknowledge the recurrent themes identified through research.

In applying the term "maternal outcasts" to mothers who have had their children removed from their care, Broadhurst and Mason (2013, p. 296) describe the mothers' situation as a "by-product of modern child protection systems that are adept at identifying and safeguarding many children, but less able to respond to the continuing needs of parents".

In their paper aiming to capture the consequences of court-ordered child removal, Broadhurst and Mason (2017, pp. 41–42) outline five specific consequences, namely grief, social and legal stigmatisation, welfare penalties and third-party ripple effects.

Similarly, Memarnia et al. (2015, pp. 311–314) discuss trauma, disenfranchised grief, child protection proceedings, spoilt identities, support systems and historical background as primary themes.

In a Welsh study of women working with third-sector support services, all women were reported to be suffering from mental health problems, 33% reported previously experiencing domestic violence, 40% reported substance use, 60% were not in any education, employment or training, and 73% were experiencing debt problems (Roberts, Maxwell, Messenger & Palmer, 2018, pp. 21–23).

## *Disenfranchised Grief*

In his book *Disenfranchised Grief: Recognizing Hidden Sorrow*, Doka defines disenfranchised grief as "grief connected to loss which cannot be openly acknowledged, publicly mourned or socially supported" (Doka, 1989, p. 4). As such, "either the relationship is not recognised, the loss is not recognised or the griever is not recognised" (Doka, 1989, pp. 5–6). It brings focus to the "social rules that govern what losses one grieves, how one grieves them, who legitimately can grieve loss and how to and to whom others respond with sympathy and support" (Doka, 2017, p. 378).

Robinson (2007, p. 8) describes how many mothers in Australia are told that they are "doing the right thing" in giving up their children and as such "there is no reason to be sad" and that these discourses, along with "getting over it" and "moving on with their lives", reinforce the "denial of the legitimacy of their grief".

In their study attempting to capture the experience of birth mothers who have been through recurrent care proceedings, Broadhurst et al. (2017, pp. 101–2) describe complex grief responses as a result of the children being psychologically present but physically absent, the disagreement with the decision of removal, the difficulties in finding distractions through work or education and the resultant isolation and shame.

In the same study, a mother described her experience as "absolutely heartbreaking" with a sense of loss that "never leaves you" with "reminders everywhere" (Broadhurst et al., 2017, p. 75). One mother described the contemplation of suicide, saying "I've got nothing left." Another mother described a sense of hopelessness and the return to using substances to "forget what you're going through" (Broadhurst et al., 2017, p. 75). It was concluded within this study that "without exception" these mothers experienced "an acute sense of loss when their children were removed from their care" and that this loss is "enduring and very difficult to resolve" (Broadhurst et al., 2017, p. 74).

## *Childhood, Relationships and Trauma*

It has been reported that these mothers have often experienced high levels of maltreatment and abuse, as well as a lack of emotional stability and neglect in their own childhoods, with many having been through the care system themselves (Broadhurst et al., 2017, pp. 292, 59).

In an English analysis of 354 mothers who had more than one child removed from their care, there were significantly high levels of adverse childhood experiences (ACEs) reported (Broadhurst et al., 2017, p. 25). Specifically, 56% reported having an ACE score of 4 or more, 66% reported experiencing neglect, 67% reported emotional abuse, 52% reported physical abuse, 53% reported sexual abuse, and 40% had been in care themselves (Broadhurst et al., 2017, p. 25). This final statistic is reinforced by a Welsh study that found that 27% of birth mothers and 19% of birth fathers whose children had been placed for adoption had experiences of being in care themselves (Roberts, Meakings, Forrester, Smith & Shelton, 2017, p. 25).

It is important to note here that these experiences of abuse both emotionally and physically extend into these mothers' adulthood. There does not appear to be much inquiry or research into these mothers' adult experiences of abuse, specifically within relationships. The stories presented here all include significant and traumatic experiences of domestic abuse and violence within relationships, which is important to identify and acknowledge.

These adverse and traumatic experiences, not only through childhood but also into adulthood, are then compounded with the additional trauma of having their children removed from their care. Memarnia et al. (2015, p. 309) reported that all the mothers interviewed in their study described "intense shock and disbelief after their children were removed" and all described "coping through avoidance of their emotions, of people and places that reminded them of their children, and of friends and family". As such it is important to acknowledge these mothers' historical and present experiences of abuse, as well as their experiences of disconnectedness, avoidance and withdrawal, and to be able to contextualise this as trauma.

## *Social Penalties, Stigmatisation and Repeated Removals*

It is often the case that parents who appear before the family courts are lone mothers receiving welfare benefits as their primary income and many living in social housing (Broadhurst & Mason, 2017, p. 52). Once the decision for child removal has been finalised, these women can experience a number of critical issues associated with their welfare and housing entitlements including benefit change and instability, often creating debt, which in turn increases the risk of homelessness (Broadhurst & Mason, 2017, pp. 52–53).

Specifically, in my experience of working with women in Wales, after the removal of their children, they are often left in three-bedroom houses, which are not only far too big and expensive for them but also serve as a constant reminder of their children's absence. Additionally, they are no longer eligible for Child Tax Credits and need to be changed onto Universal Credit, which can result in benefit delays and significant tax credit debts if the payment is continued for longer than it should have been. This financial instability can then have a significant knock-on effect on their housing stability, often resulting in rent arrears and possible evictions. This, in short, is making vulnerable women even more vulnerable.

In addition to these social penalties, many women report feelings of being "nailed to the past" by a "non-erasable history" (Broadhurst & Mason, 2017, p. 50; Broadhurst et al., 2017, p. 82). For parents whose children have been removed through a court order, a "non-erasable family court record" can lead to ongoing experiences of feeling "harshly judged" and stigmatised during any subsequent services involvement, which in turn leads to a sense of "caution", "mistrust" and "unfairness" regarding services involvement in their lives (Broadhurst & Mason, 2017, p. 50; Broadhurst et al., 2017, p. 82).

This social and legal stigmatisation has a significant effect on these mothers being able to remain caring for additional children they may have after previous children have been removed. Although many infants are removed from their parents at birth, there is minimal literature to date regarding this topic (Broadhurst et al., 2017, p. 83).

## Narrative Practices

*"...the typical form of framing experience (and our memory of it) is in narrative form, and...what does not get structured narratively suffers loss in memory." (Bruner, 1990, p. 56)*

The intention of this section is to briefly introduce the theoretical underpinnings and associated research of specific narrative practices that informed the development and presentation of the following stories.

In her literature review of support services for birth parents having gone through adoption processes, Neil (2017, p. 23) identified narrative therapy as a therapeutic intervention to treat trauma symptoms. Similarly, Memarnia et al. (2015, p. 316) outline the potential usefulness of narrative approaches with birth mothers whose children have been adopted. They stated that narrative approaches could give mothers the opportunity to re-author their stories and reduce distress associated with disenfranchised grief (p. 316).

These narrative practices have been developed and implemented in Australia within organisations supporting mothers who have had children removed from their care. Specifically, Evelyn Robinsons (2002), both a counsellor and mother who lost a child through adoption processes has undertaken and given accounts of narrative-based therapeutic approaches used within a group context to support mothers experiencing disenfranchised grief.

### *Collective Narrative Practice*

In his seminal book *Collective Narrative Practices*, Denborough (2008, pp. 27–28) focuses on "the use of collective narrative documentation as a response to collective trauma", with this approach being used in numerous contexts, including women experiencing grief and mothers whose children have been removed from their care.

Denborough states that "far too often collective histories of trauma are forgotten" and that collective narrative documentation can serve as a different form of "historical testimony" that not only elicits stories of trauma but also stories of survival (Denborough, 2008, p. 42). It is through the process of telling, documenting and collecting numerous stories of hardship and perseverance that not only attempts to give a voice to underprivileged storytellers but also creates a context for meaningful and personal contribution to others experiencing similar hardship (pp. 40–44).

### *Narrative Timelines*

Narrative timelines have been developed in a number of different contexts in numerous ways. In continuation from collective narrative practices, Denborough (2008, pp. 144–159) outlines the methodology of collective narrative timelines and maps of history. Through this methodology, practitioners are able to construct and share detailed timelines that trace personal histories in a way that powerfully honour their experiences as well as contribute to a collective sense of purpose and acknowledgment (p. 144).

Similarly, Schauer, Neuner and Elbert (2011, p. 34) have developed Narrative Exposure Therapy, which uses narrative timelines to not only focus on reducing symptoms of trauma but also focuses on the reconstruction of autobiographical memory and consistency in one's life narrative. This construction of consistency or coherence in one's narrative has been identified as relating significantly to psychological well-being, specifically in terms of one's sense of identity and social relationships, as well as one's sense of purpose and meaning in life (Waters & Fivush, 2015).

### *Re-membering*

Using the metaphor of "saying hullo again", Michael White (1988, p. 18) attempted to bring to question dominant discourses regarding grief, such as "saying goodbye", "accepting the loss", "getting on with life" as well as categorisations such as "pathological", "delayed" or "failed" grief. The focus was intentionally shifted from "grief work" towards an invitation to reclaim and recount specific and cherished experiences of these important relationships.

This practice has been referred to as Re-membering. The concept of Re-membering was first introduced by Barbra Myerhoff (1982, p. 111), as:

"...calling attention to the reaggregation of members, the figures who belong to one's life story, one's own prior selves, as well as significant others who are part of the story. Re-membering...is a purposive, significant unification... [in which] life is given a shape that extends back in the past and forward into the future."

In integrating this concept into therapeutic practice, White (2007, p. 129) details how an individual's identity can be revised and reconstructed through an "association of life" which is composed of significant and influential figures from one's past, present and projected future who collectively contribute to one's own sense of identity. Re-membering conversations have the intention of developing a "multivoiced" sense of identity through emphasising the contribution of others (Myerhoff, p. 111; White, p. 138).

## *Re-authoring*

In analysing the theoretical underpinnings of "story grammar", Bruner (1986, p. 14) describes the presence of two distinct landscapes: the landscape of action and the landscape of consciousness. In adopting this dichotomy, Epston and White (1992, p. 123) detail that the landscape of action consists of "events that are linked together...through a temporal dimension according to specific plots". Contrastingly, the landscape of consciousness consists of the meanings derived through the reflection on such events, which can determine what these events say about the desires, preferences, goals, values, beliefs, intentions or commitments of an individual (Epston & White, 1992, p. 124; White, 1995, p. 31).

In applying theory to practice, White (1995, p. 31) explains how when individuals come to therapy, they often give an account of the "landscape of action of the dominant story". To engage in a re-authoring conversation then is to attempt to move between both landscapes with the intention of developing an alternative storyline in contrast to the dominant, often deficit-focused narrative and allowing the individual to derive new conclusions about their life (White, 2007, p. 83).

## *Primary Authorship*

This final narrative practice I deem to be the most important and the one that takes precedence over the others. It is a political practice that aims to address what Pupavac (2001, p. 367) coined "therapeutic governance", the way that "psychosocial and therapeutic programs inadvertently impose certain understandings of life, trauma and healing".

In an attempt to address this governance or position of power, White (2005, p. 9) developed a "decentred but influential" positioning of the therapist. He defines *decentred* as "according priority to the personal stories of each individual, giving them *'primary authorship status'* and taking into consideration their own personal insider skills and knowledges" (p. 9). Additionally, he defines *influential* as using reflective questioning to scaffold and help individuals to richly develop the alternative stories of their lives (Gaddis, 2016, p. 12; White, 2005, p. 9).

In this way, a therapist is advised to avoid assuming a privileged position, by resisting to act upon the convictions of "how things ought to be" based on taken-for-granted truths, and instead work respectfully with an individual to assist them to activate their own knowledge, strengths and resources that reflect their own personal culture, ideologies and intentions (Rober & Seltzer, 2010, pp. 125–127).

With the intention of addressing my own position of power and adopting a decentred position, my real name has been withheld, just like the mothers whose stories are presented. This is so my education, my profession and my privilege do not mask the mothers' voices, which are the primary authors of this text.

In concluding, and in reinforcing this position, I would like to end the introduction with two specific quotes. The first is from Schauer, Neuner and Elbert (2010) regarding working with patients who have experienced significant trauma:

"The therapist does not interpret for the patient. The patient is the authority regarding her/his own experience. Therefore, the therapist does not need to agree with the content of what is being said or the way the patient interprets the experiences. The therapist must simply agree to accept it as the patient's truth and the world." (p. 72)

Finally, a quote from D. Hughes (1997), a mother who had her child placed into adoption, and who wrote a personal account of her experience of counselling:

"...the most valuable and meaningful thing...that a counsellor can do for a birthmother...is to accept the pain we experience without escaping into the notion that this can somehow be made better." (p. 9)

# The (Horror) Story

*Rachel Alby*

19

My name is Rachel. I was born in June 1989. I have an older sister, Jessica; a younger brother, James; and a younger sister, Kelly.

One of my earliest memories is of when I was about four years old and James was two. Our Mum took Kelly, who was a baby then, and left James and I in the bath. We never saw her again. I have never seen her since.

The police eventually came and took us to our Nan's place. This was my father's mother. Our Nan decided to keep Jessica and sent James and I to our father's house where he lived with his partner, our stepmother. They also had children of their own. I never have really understood why our Nan only took care of our sister. She knew that our father was abusive, and really, she should have protected us. I still hold some resentment towards her for that.

My father and stepmother were abusive, towards each other, and us. They beat us, frequently, daily. I had witnessed frequently my father threaten us and others with knives.

When I was about eight years old, I watched my father stamp on the back of a guy's head which was on the road. I still have that image in my memory. I still have a lot of horrific images in my memory.

There was lots of drinking and lots of drug use. My father would sell a lot of drugs. We would often find him passed out on the bathroom floor. As kids we would take his money or drugs and try to make our own money. He used to put drugs in our pillowcases and get us to sleep over at people's houses. We didn't know these people. We had never met them before, and we were left with them, overnight, sometimes for days.

The final straw was when my father broke my jaw. I was about ten years old. My brother had been in trouble because he had done something at school. I tried to protect him from being beaten, and my father broke my jaw.

My father died last year. The same day I lost my youngest child. My stepmother still lives in the area I grew up. I still see her now and again.

When we were young, I had to look after my brother. I tried. Our favourite times were when we used to order pizza. I would get veggie supreme, always, and James would get something with meat, usually pepperoni.

I was ten when I put myself into foster care. It was the best decision I have ever made. I begged my brother to come with me. He was so young. He didn't understand and didn't know what to do. I think he still holds some resentment towards me for leaving him with our father and stepmother.

I went into a foster family. They were lovely. My foster parents were called Lily and Oli. His real name was Oliver, but we all called him Oli. Lily has just recently moved to England, and Oli died last year. They had three children of their own. They also had two other foster kids and me. It was a big household.

It was around this time my father got put in prison. My brother eventually did go into foster care when he was about twelve. His foster carer was really lovely.

I remember drug use started pretty early with me. I was about eight when I had my first spliff. It was around then I started smoking cigarettes.

By the time I was twelve I was drinking alcohol and using all sorts of drugs. I had a perspective of trying anything once. I started using ecstasy and base, LSD and ketamine at this age. I only really stopped at about twenty-one when my first child, Derek, was born.

## School Years

A year before I went into foster care, when I was about nine, I got kicked out of primary school for breaking a kid's ribs. He had hit my brother, so I hit him back.

Even before this we weren't allowed on the school premises during break times like recess and lunch. My father would have to come and pick us up and drop us off.

I went to another primary school after this.

High school wasn't much better. I went to three different high schools. I got kicked out of the first one because I threw a chair at a teacher. I got them in the head too.

I then went to an all-girls school. But I guess that didn't stop me from getting into fights. I remember getting in trouble for punching a girl who had said something nasty about my foster mum.

I was here the longest of all my schools. I was naughty, that is how I would describe myself there. I was naughty and I was a bitch.

The last high school I went to, the other students used to call me 'Heady'. It meant that I was messed up in the head. Part of me thinks this is true.

I did like art at school. I remember I made this giant artwork that was a fabric dragon with a large red background. I put a lot of work into that, and it turned out really good.

I used to love history and learning about the wars. I still do. Anything to do with the World Wars I am really interested in. I read a lot about the wars. I also really like reading true crime novels.

## My Best Friend, Emma

My best friend was Emma. We have been friends since I was ten. We met up at the train station in Bridgend. She gave me a fag. Since then, we were best friends. She even gave me my first phone.

We didn't go to school together—she went to a Welsh school—but we hung out all the time. I became part of her family. We spent a lot of time hanging out with her brother and his partner.

She was my best friend. We helped each other raise our children.

We haven't spoken to each other since my previous partner got convicted. I think she feels guilt for what happened to my children as well.

She used to look after me. I used to look after her. We looked after each other. I do miss Emma.

## My Relationships

I had a number of long-term relationships growing up. Most of which seemed to be named Matthew. The first was with Matthew S when I was fourteen years old; he was twenty-four. We were together for approximately four years.

I ended up cheating on him with Matthew K when I was seventeen, and I ended up in a relationship with him for two years. He was thirty-two at the time. This wasn't the best situation as he was my aunty's boyfriend and I had started sleeping with him. He was also the father of my first child, Derek.

The next relationship I had was when I was twenty; he was twenty-eight at the time. His name was Matthew W. I was with him for six years. He is the father of two of my children, Cerys and Sian.

He was a tattooist. We met when he was giving me my first tattoo. He has given me most of my tattoos. We ended up living together. To begin with he was really good to me. He was caring and we really looked after each other.

Eventually, over time, he became controlling. There were occasions when he locked me in the bedroom for periods of time.

## The Older Three Children

### *Derek*

Derek was born in May 2010. I had Derek when I was twenty. Matthew W knew he wasn't the father but was okay with it and didn't seem to care. The pregnancy and having Derek were just brilliant, although he really didn't want to come out.

He developed a serious medical condition. During this time, he was in hospital for two weeks, then moved to another hospital for another three weeks, and then had to go to hospital every two weeks after that.

This was difficult. Very difficult. I remember having some problems with doctors during this time and getting really impatient with them. But we got through it.

I remember when Derek was really little, Matthew's sister took the three of us to London with her family. It was lovely. We went sightseeing and had some great food. Derek got spoilt rotten.

I would describe Derek as inspiring. He gives everything, always 100%. He is cheeky but also very caring and helpful.

It was around this time I got a job. I was working at a fish shop. I loved it. It was nice to have some income then, and we could go on trips.

*Dear Derek,*

*When God gave you to me, he knew that I needed you. He gave us five amazing years together. It was just you, me, and your dad. When your sister Cerys finally came along, you were so happy to finally be a big brother. You held her and helped Mummy to read and play with her. You used to help with bath time, and now she is almost four years old. You used to love playing games. You didn't always get along, but I know you still love her and your other siblings as well. You have always been a lovely brother.*

*You used to love going to school to learn and play with your friends. You used to love going on day trips with the nursery and school. You were a very smart and loving boy.*

*You used to challenge me in so many ways, and you used to teach me about things I never knew I'd be interested in. I used to love when you came out of school and see the way you would light up when you had learnt something new. You were such a lovely son, brother and friend.*

*You used to love to crawl into bed with me and your dad in the morning, and you used to love to brush my hair. You would love to sing songs and read books. You used to play with dinosaurs as well as trains. You loved to go on walks with me and Aunty Diane. You loved animals. I remember the first time me and your dad took you to a farm. You were so happy and were just running around and feeding the animals and playing in the park. You used to love the swing and always tell me to push you higher.*

*I can't tell you how much of my heart you fill. But I can tell you how empty I am without you. I wish I could have seen you grow up. There was always something special about our relationship that we had. I was twenty-one when you were born, and it was one of the best days of my life. I hope I was a good mum to you over the time we had together. I know I haven't always been a perfect mum to you and your sister, and I am very sorry for this.*

*I just wanted you to know how much I love you. You will always be in my heart. I miss you every day and life is hard without you in it. Thank you for helping me with your chores and when I needed assistance with your sister. Thank you for being patient with me and for accepting my apologies, I hope.*

*You are incredible. Never forget that, and never forget that I will always be here for you if you ever need me.*

*I love you loads and loads, Derek.*

*Mummy Rachel.*

**Cerys**

Cerys was born in September 2011. I had Cerys when I was twenty-two. She was nine pounds, eleven and a half ounces. The pregnancy was great, until towards the end when she cracked my ribs.

Cerys was born with a hearing problem and was in intensive care for a week after she was born. She was okay but suffered serious hearing loss. We brought her to our new home we had moved into around this time.

Derek used to find it really difficult to sleep sometimes and would get very overwhelmed. This occasionally resulted in him and Cerys fighting and not getting along.

Despite this, there was an understanding between the two of them, and Derek was very good at knowing what Cerys was trying to communicate and often acted as an interpreter to let us know what Cerys wanted.

We used to call Cerys 'Rugby'. She loves to eat and eats anything and everything. She loves being outdoors, running around parks and getting muddy.

*Dear Cerys,*

*I dreamed of you for three years. I thought I would never have a girl after Derek was born. But you finally came into our lives, and you were so worth the wait.*

*The nurses brought you to me in a red and white sleepy suit and a red bow in your hair. I had never seen anything so beautiful in the entire world. You made our family complete. Little did I know that in the next two years you would have more siblings. You were an amazing big sister. You used to love to help feed your sister and help with feeding the dog and going on walks. You have an innate ability to be nurturing and loving.*

*I have to admit you're more stubborn and hard-headed than your other siblings. Your dad always said the same thing. This toughness will be an asset to you as you grow older. But I pray it will not become a stumbling block in your life. I know my own stubborn tendencies have caused me some trouble over the years.*

*You are strong and beautiful, and you have such a sweet and caring heart. On one Christmas Eve, you put cookies and milk out for Santa, but when Mum had come back in you had eaten the cookies and drunk the milk. You used to love the outdoors as well as your food. You could eat anything.*

*My relationship with you is so different than what I had with your brother. Sometimes we would clash, but I think that was just a girl thing. I hope that you know that I love you so incredibly much. My life is empty without you. You made me smile and laugh every day. You made me so proud of you in everything you did. You made my heart do flip-flops when I saw you helping your brother and sister and when you would dance around the house. You are everything that is good in the world.*

*I hope you are proud to have me as your mum. I know I haven't always been a great mum. I want to be, but unfortunately, I may never get that chance now. But I promise I will make you proud of me one day, because no matter what, I will always be proud to call you my daughter. I love you, Sweetheart.*

*Love you loads,*

*Mummy Rachel.*

## *Sian*

Sian was born in February 2013 when I was twenty-three years old. She was lovely and quiet. She was lactose intolerant, which made mealtimes that were already difficult even more difficult.

The way I would describe her is that she was literally attached to my hip. The thing I liked most about her was her smile and laugh. She had this little chuckle that was just heart-warming. She was only two when she was removed from my care.

*Dear Sian,*

*The day I found out you were joining our family I was so happy and so was all our family. I couldn't believe I was blessed with another child, and your dad was over the moon. I couldn't wait to hold you in my arms.*

*From the day you were born you were so laid-back and quiet. You used to sleep through the night. You would only cry if you were ill or your skin was bad. It used to break my heart seeing you like that.*

*You used to love it when we all sang Twinkle Twinkle Little Star. You used to love all music and light-up toys. You used to love watching your brother and sister playing with their toys. You used to love it when Derek would play peek-a-boo with you. I remember your first word being Dad.*

*I remember you loved it when we took you to the indoor playground. You loved the ball pit and when I took you down the slide. I remember when we took you to see Father Christmas for the first time, but you didn't like that.*

*You loved our dog Ben and you loved going in the car, although you would often fall asleep. You loved your door bouncer as well.*

*I love everything about you. You were wonderful in every way possible. Just like your brother and your sister.*

*I remember it being hard when you went on to solid foods as you had a milk allergy, but you loved your veg and fruit and especially breadsticks.*

*I can remember your first time in the park. You loved the slide but hated the swings. Your first birthday was amazing. We had a little tea party, and all your family came, and you loved the big doll we got you. Your first Christmas was very special. You loved all the lights and loved all the wrapping paper. I remember you loved it when we took you to the Coca-Cola truck.*

*You loved it when we took you to Folly Farm. You loved to help Mum feed the giraffes and you loved to play in the sand. You loved your monkey teddy.*

*I remember we took you to meet your aunty and she loved you. I miss you so much. It gets hard and it breaks my heart thinking that I won't get to see you grow up, but I think about you, your brother and sisters every day.*

*I love you loads and loads,*

*Mummy Rachel.*

## The Best Times with the Kids

We used to have a lot of fun. We used to have great parties! I remember a Halloween party we had one year. I dressed up as Jack Skellington from *The Nightmare Before Christmas*, Cerys dressed up as a devil and Derek wanted to be a princess.

At that party there were twenty-eight kids. It was hectic. There were a number of parents, and we took it in turns to manage the kids. Some took them all trick-or-treating, and I set up games like bobbing for apples. I remember making a pirate cake.

I remember we used to get old records and heat them up and make bowls out of them. Then we would have record-bowl painting parties for Cerys.

I remember we had a sludge pool party! That was amazing!

There was a time when we covered the playroom with flour so we could make flour angels. Flour ended up everywhere and it took me forever to clean it all up, but it was worth it.

I remember I went dressed up as Spider-Man to the kid's school for Derek's birthday once. There were kids everywhere and they wouldn't let me leave. It took me over an hour to get out of the school. I remember dressing up as Tigger as well.

I used to love baking cakes for them. I still love to bake. The cake I am most proud of was a three-tier princess cake that was purple and pink and had smarties coming out of the centre. It took me two days to make.

The other cake I am most proud of was a dinosaur cake. It was a T-Rex. It was an all-green sponge cake with green liquid that came out when you cut it. That also took two days to make.

*Dear Derek, Cerys, and Sian,*

*This is a letter for all of you. I know I was never a perfect mum. But I did my best. I wish every day that I could turn back time, but I can't. I don't agree with social services and the judge's decisions, and I will never forgive your dad, and I am sorry that our family got torn apart.*

*I should have paid more attention to what was going on, but I never thought your dad would hurt you in that way. I failed to protect you and failed as a mum because I didn't keep you safe, and I will never forgive myself for that.*

*I hope one day you will forgive me. I want you to know that I love you with all my heart and I promise I will make it up to you. I love you so much and so does your dad, even though he did wrong.*

*If you have any questions, I promise I will answer them. I will never ever stop thinking about you, and I will always say good morning and good night to you. I know you are with a loving family, but I want you to know that you also have another family that loves you with all their hearts.*

*I love you loads and loads,*
*Mummy Rachel.*

## At Folly Farm One Day and Life Ruined the Next

I think it was sometime in April 2014. It might have been earlier. The police came and knocked on my front door. I was making dinner. Matthew answered the door. The police took him straight away. The kids and I were asked to go upstairs, and we stayed there until Emma came and took the kids with her for the night.

Two weeks later the police came and asked for Matthew's laptop, any memory sticks and devices he had. I gave it all to them. Eventually, they told me that he apparently had billions of indecent images and videos of children and teenagers over categories A, B and C. There were four videos involving Cerys. I was eventually told what was in these videos. He is now in prison.

Initially, he was given bail for two weeks. At that point they had not found the videos of Cerys, and he had contact with her during this time. I thought this was horrendous, and Cerys did not want to see him. I did threaten the social worker with a machete over this. I had a mental breakdown once I found out.

We were at Folly Farm one day, and our life was ruined the next.

I started smoking weed a lot at this time. I didn't know how else to cope. I was really down. I didn't know what to do. I wanted to try and talk to the children about what had happened. But I didn't even know how to process what had happened myself. I didn't know how to explain to them what had happened. I didn't know how to talk to them about what they had been through.

I had horrible thoughts. I thought that it would be best just to kill us all. I even got to the point of buying a gun off eBay. I couldn't cope anymore. I would never have hurt my children. I would have hurt myself but not my children. Finally, I went to the doctors and asked for help.

The children were taken into foster care in August 2014. It was just after Cerys' birthday. I can be feisty, and I didn't want them to go. It took ten police officers and three social workers to get those children out of the house. They gave me more time with them because they had to call for more police to come.

Derek is in foster care. Cerys is in the process of getting an adoption order. Sian is adopted. Derek and Cerys still get to see each other.

## The Black Room

After I lost the children, I spent seven months in my bedroom. I painted the whole room black. The only person I had contact with during this time was my drug dealer. He would do all my shopping for me. I was using large amounts of alcohol, cannabis, speed, coke and diazepam. I would just sit and watch DVDs. I missed contact with the children.

No one tried to help. No one knew how hard it was for me. No one even really knew I was there. I just wasn't there.

## Ethan and His Mum Holly

Eventually, a mutual friend of my drug dealer, Ethan, and his mother Holly found out about me and how hard I was finding life. They helped and supported me.

Ethan literally picked me up and took me out of my bedroom. I stayed at their house for a week. They cooked for me and tried to get me to put on some weight. I slowly regained some contact with the world.

When I went back home, they would come and visit every day. They didn't have to do that for me. I am sure if they had to do it all over again, they would. I guess, at least to them, I am worth the effort.

During this time, I was still smoking a lot of cannabis. Ethan and I developed a relationship. We weren't really a couple, more just friends with benefits.

## The Younger Two Children

### *Evelyn*

Evelyn was born in July 2015. I had moved to live closer to my family. I had more support that way. I lived by myself in a one-bedroom council flat.

Evelyn was born when I was twenty-six years old. Ethan was the father. Evelyn was taken from me at birth. She is now adopted.

### *Chloe*

Chloe was born in September 2016. I had Chloe when I was twenty-seven. Matthew K, who I dated when I was seventeen and had stayed with for two weeks at the beginning of 2016, was the father. There was a DNA test proving that Alex, my partner at the time, wasn't Chloe's father, so it must have been Matthew.

Three days after I had Chloe, she was taken into foster care and now she is adopted. The same day, my father died. That was a horrible day. Although my dad was abusive when I was young, once I had the children, he was different. He was there and supported us a lot. He loved his grandchildren and our relationship got so much better. I lost my daughter and my dad in the same day.

## The End of 2016 and the Start of 2017

After I had Evelyn and she was taken from me, I spent a lot of time getting wasted. I met Alex on a dating app and we started seeing each other. Alex is a convicted murderer.

We were using a lot of drugs. We started using the legal high (now illegal) Spice daily. On top of this was lots of cannabis, hash and speed use.

While I was with Alex, there was a time when I went and stayed with Matthew K for two weeks. I then went back to stay with Alex.

When he found out that I had been with Matthew, he beat me up. I was pregnant with Chloe at the time. He was arrested because of this.

I then moved back to stay with Ethan and his mother Holly and then eventually went to stay with my friend Jenny, who I was living with when I had Chloe.

## Aerosol Cans, Homelessness and Sam

After I had lost Chloe, I went to stay with Matthew K again, briefly. I then met Jamie and lived with him for three months.

We were smoking a lot of cannabis, and this is when I started using aerosol cans. From the beginning of 2017, I was using about thirty aerosol cans a day. I used that many until I started to try and reduce my use at the end of May.

I left Jamie after we had a physical argument. During that argument he slapped me. I then threw him down the stairs, then picked him up and threw him into a mirror.

After that event I stayed with my stepmum for two days and then needed to move out. I was homeless.

This is when I met Sam. We met through a homeless support service, and we started seeing each other. During this time, I got put into a B and B through the council. I was there for three weeks until I got kicked out. Sam had moved and was staying with me there when he shouldn't have been. One of the other residents attacked him, and then I attacked them. We were now homeless again.

We stayed at the train station for three nights. I remember it being rainy and wet. I remember waking up and feeling so shameful in the morning when people came onto the platform to go to work. We then stayed in the doorway of a closed-down shop for nearly two to three months. It was depressing and scary living there. We would have drunk people screaming at us or trying to get under our tarpaulin. It was shameful; people would look at us. I just wanted to give up.

It was there where we had sex for the first time. This was a big step. It was hard to build a relationship with Sam. I had been suffering from depression and was burnt out. I was cold towards other people and didn't want them to touch me at all. I didn't want to be hurt again. I had been hurt so many times before. It was just my life. I didn't really understand why he would be interested in me. He said he would help take care of me and keep me safe. He helped fill a hole in my life, and our relationship became the first real connection I had with anyone for years.

There was a time I was using aerosol cans on the doorstep of the shop. Sam tried to put a tarpaulin up for me. I had used cans in so many places in public, like the public bus stops, the library, carparks, even in a Tesco toilet before I left the store. I really didn't care or think about what I was doing.

Eventually, we got a tent and we moved to what we called 'the farm', which was in a forest not far out of town. We lived in that tent for nearly five months.

## Months in the Tent

Living in a tent in the forest was horrible at times. When the weather was bad, everything would get wet. Our bedding would get wet, and our clothes, and we had no way of drying them until the weather got better. We had to pee and shit in the woods just like animals. No one seemed to care if we lived or died.

Not only that, there were a number of times when teenagers or people who we'd had fallings out with in the past would come and either steal or destroy our things. We had a group of teenagers set one of our tents on fire, so we had to get another one.

There were some okay times though. We would see a lot of animals and wildlife around. We saw a lot of bugs! Once we saw a caterpillar that looked just like a little dragon. We saw foxes and squirrels, and Sam said he saw a peacock once.

We used to try our best cooking things on the fire. I tried to cook fishcakes one time. I got rather frustrated with them and ended up throwing them in the fire. Sam tried to salvage them, and they didn't turn out too bad in the end. The best meal we had was ribs that we had cooked on the fire. One day, Sam and I would like to write a book on how to cook on a fire when you are homeless.

## Accidental Fires and Decreasing Cans

There were a few times when using cans became really dangerous. There was once when Sam and I were playing Monopoly in the tent. I had been using cans probably ten minutes before Sam tried to light a cigarette. I basically just caught on fire, and the flames went all the way up my arms, over my face and mouth and burnt my hair. I then passed out and came to about ten minutes later. This terrified both of us, especially Sam as he didn't mean to do it. This wasn't the first time I had accidently set fire to myself because of can use, but it definitely made me seriously think about decreasing.

I had been using cans since November, and by May I had decided that I would have to start decreasing. This would have to be gradual. By the beginning of July, I had come down from thirty cans a day to fifteen, and by mid-July I was averaging about eight a day. I had a few really rough days in August when I used about thirty cans, but mostly I averaged around six cans. Come September, we were given a flat to move into through a housing association. I really did not want to be using cans in my new house and I was determined to stop when I moved in. The moving day was really stressful, and I ended up using fifteen cans. But the next day was my first day without any cans since November, and I have not used any cans since. This has been so hard, and every day is so difficult, but I remind myself I have to do it.

## Getting a House

Finally getting a house was great, despite it being in the middle of nowhere. Much better than being in a tent, that is for sure! I really appreciate now having a solid roof over my head and having an actual bed to sleep in. It's nice to actually have a bath! I do love my baths.

We can actually charge our phones and my tablet without leaving them at a charity organisation. It's nice to have a TV. I haven't had a TV in so long. I have really enjoyed getting back into documentaries and extreme cake-making shows. I have been going down to the local library as well.

It is still difficult, though. We don't have any white goods, which makes things really hard. We still can't really cook, and we don't have a way of washing our clothes yet. We are still working on getting this sorted.

## The Future

We are organising our Universal Credit and making sure we are managing our money better. I have gotten in contact with substance use services and try to drop in and see them weekly. I also have some mental health support and have a worker who I am also trying to see weekly. I have been colouring and have a rather large collection of colouring books now. It is one way to keep my mind off things and keep me busy. I would also really like to try and do some work in the future. That is important to me. I don't mind if it is voluntary or not. I would really like to stay where we are.

Moving forward, there are still a lot of things to be sorted out, especially about our housing and finances, and for me to manage my substance use and mental health difficulties. I have recently got a brain scan done because I have been experiencing fits more frequently. We thought this had to do with my epilepsy, but it turns out there is a small tumour in my brain that is causing it. We'll just keep dealing with this as it progresses. There is always something to make the story worse. If it isn't one thing, there is always another.

I've got a cat to look after now. Her name is Hope. I like our house, and looking over the valley is really lovely. It is still going to be hard going moving forward, but I will just have to keep at it.

*Dear Rachel,*

*Where do I start? I remember the first time I met you. It was in a forest by a tent. You had to get quickly changed because you didn't think you were dressed well enough to go out. We then went down to McDonald's, and I began to hear about you and the situation you were living in.*

*I remember hearing of how long you had been homeless for, the struggle of getting through each day and how aerosol cans were helping you do that but at the same time putting your life at risk. Most of all I remember hearing just how much you missed having your children in your life.*

*I believed from the beginning, and still believe now, that you deserve a better life than living in a tent with aerosol cans. I think you now believe that also, and I have seen you day after day attempt to make your life better. It has been inspiring to watch you work as hard as you have. In three months, I watched you independently, and with very little support, decrease your can use, and not only find a house, but turn it into a home.*

*I feel privileged not only to have met you but that you were willing to share your story with me. Most importantly, I would like to say thank you. I have learnt a lot from you, and through your stories and letters, others will learn and be inspired by you in the same way.*

*You are honest, strong and unrelenting, and although such attributes can sometimes get you in trouble, most of the time they are an asset, and demonstrate the genuine care you have for others. I only hope you can continue to develop such care and consideration for yourself.*

*I hope that the future that lies before you is filled with warmth and security. Things won't be perfect, and often they will be just plain difficult. But if there is a person that I know who can get through horrendous times alive and still maintain a sense of smart-arse humour it is you.*

*I sincerely hope you are able to find a way to move from loving your children in their presence to continually loving them in their absence. They are an important part of your life which deserves acknowledgment.*

*In the meantime, I only hope you take the time to cherish moments of joy, no matter how small and few. They will be there, hidden amongst the ruins.*

*I wish you all the best for the future.*

*Please take care.*

*Warmly,*

*Lewis*



37

# Second Chances and Parallels

*Lydia Bailey*

Kinda nervous.

Have never shown anyone my writing. Or had it analysed or scrutinised in any way.

Most of it we have touched on but, as you quickly picked up, my stories don't really go chronologically, and to understand one story, you need to know the background to another.

Has been a help writing this. Sometimes spend hours just letting it all out. Enjoy the read, and welcome to my head!

## 4th March 2019 – 7:45 p.m.
## Room 6

Had the crappy news that they are going to hostel swap me when I woke up yesterday.

Usually, I would be in bits, crying my eyes out at the injustice of it all, but at the moment I don't seem to have any overwhelming emotion about it.

There have been some awful times, but they taught me the most and sometimes were the reason the good things that followed happened.

No mistakes, just lessons.

I have been near death too many times for there not to be a reason I'm still here.

Sometimes I would feel invisible, and it seemed the worse I felt the less people could see me. I'd walk through a city centre with tears streaming down my face and not one person asked if I was okay.

It was the same when I had a black eye. That was an odd experience. I really felt people looked down on me. I felt really ashamed when I was around others, oddly enough.

I remember a lot of stares and people looking at me like I was dangerous, but really looking down their noses at me. Not once do I remember a sympathetic look or smile.

Regardless of what I do or how I do it, it will always seem to be wrong. I always seem to be the scapegoat or made an example of. This sounds negative, but thinking back, it's done me a world of good. It's kind of reassuring to prove that even when I follow the rules and procedures, for some reason I always seem to come off worst. I have always found it hard to turn a blind eye. Choosing my battles is something I'm struggling with.

The other night when the girls fought outside, I found it so hard to not break it up. There's a line between helping others and endangering yourself. It's a hard call to make but, all things considered, they were an even match. I exercised self-preservation. Getting involved could have resulted in an eviction.

It is just a regular occurrence here really. Just the other week a guy jumped out of the second-floor window and smashed it everywhere. The police are constantly being called. One girl stole another's credit card and went on a spending spree online. The drugs are always present and there are consistent overdoses.

Now, I am being 'relocated' due to a staff member feeling uncomfortable because I called him out on having oddly personal and inappropriate relations with the residents.

I am so beyond disappointed in the staff. If anyone should have understood, it was them. I was really hurt by what they have said and what they have not done.

It is unsafe. It scares and saddens me. I could die with little to no effort, and no one would know or find out for days. For about three hours one night I had to talk myself out of topping myself. What if I had?

***Essentials to take:***

Toiletries: Toothbrush, paste, Dove soap, deodorant, moisturiser, perfume, hairdryer, shower turban, brush, clips and bobbles.

Towels: hand and shower.

Double duvet with two covers. Pink blanket. Three pillows with six covers.

Books: Novel, black pad, similar big pink one, Sudoku.

Clothes: Bed, thick grey dressing gown, thin one, long sleeve top, at least two bottoms, shorts, vest tops.

## 6th March 2019 – 4:40 a.m.
## Room 221

Since getting here two or three days ago, I have seen three kick-offs already. They had to lock down the whole reception. I just happened to be in there when they did. I just had to stay in there until it was sorted out.

I am still unsure whether I'm coping really well or not at all. Either way, it's working. I'm getting stronger. I'm enjoying the occasional good memory, rather than feeling overwhelmed with hurt.

I was unsure when you suggested talking about Rhys. I'd taken so long to lock people away. I feel abandoned by everyone who isn't in my life.

Rhys was my soulmate. He was my gay best friend. We were inseparable. We were pretty much known as 'Rhys and Lydia'; we came as a duo. What most people wouldn't have known about Rhys was just how creative he was. He was amazing on piano and played the flute and was just so creative and expressive.

I remember that his happiness was infectious. He just had this sense of fun, this shine about him. But he also had this naughty side that on first meeting him you just wouldn't expect. If he was here now, he would just comfort and support me.

He would say I am an organiser and that I am tough and sensible. He would say that I really loved him and that I was someone he could really love.

Rhys died of a heroin overdose and aneurysm when he was twenty-two. It was pretty fucked up as I had texted him the dealer's details the day before. I was on holiday when I got the text that told me he had died. My mum was there, but I remember her minimising and blaming him and not really comforting me at all. I remember the tears just streaming. It hurt. It really hurt. It was like half of my soul was just numb. I miss Rhys.

Losing people is my worst fear. I take everything personally. I feel guilty for things I haven't even done; it's weird. It is not like I am scared of dying. Dying doesn't seem so scary to me; it is living that is scary. It is living and losing people.

My mum died in 2017. I remember my dad going on a holiday instead of going to the funeral. He told me that I should go to support my brother. I was pregnant with Naomi at the time.

I was in high school when my mum's drinking started to get really bad. The responsibility fell on me to look after her. I was really struggling to keep up with school and look after her.

I remember I could never do anything right, and I remember her words to me over and over again: 'The world doesn't revolve around you.' Often, I thought she should be the one taking that advice.

I had a little sister called Daisy. She was born when I was two. She had a serious medical disease and died three months after she was born. I think my mum took this really hard but never looked for support. It is like she couldn't grieve or address any of her problems because, from what she said, she had to look after me.

I remember her saying 'I couldn't do this or that because I had to look after you.' She used to also say things like 'You are not just my daughter, you are my best friend.' This was when I was about six to ten years old. There was a real push-pull inconsistency with her. For example, she would quit smoking for us kids but then blame something we did for her starting smoking again.

I didn't go to the funeral. I remember just having a feeling of relief when she died. It was the same with my Grampy.

My Grampy was and still is really important to me. He was kind of the underdog. He was in World War II. He was placed in Burma somewhere. He was just cool and nice to me. It was the little things. That is why I liked him.

He would take me out for day trips to the park and to the bookies and to the hotels that he worked at. He would take me through the kitchens and give me food, which I just thought was great.

The thing that I learnt from him was that people aren't perfect, but in a good way. I guess this is how I developed a bit of distrust for people who appear perfect or seem like they have it all together.

It is sad when someone dies and all you are left with is a sense of relief.

My whole childhood I had been terrified of death and dying. When Rhys died my fear changed to others dying or losing more people. For a while, every time my mum left for work, I'd be terrified that would be the last time I saw her.

Rhys and I always felt bad for the Eleanor Rigbys of the world.

## 9th March 2019 – 2:44 a.m.
## Room 221

When it comes to family there's always an aftertaste or a 'but'.

All I ever got from close ones is 'I love you, *but* I don't like you' as if they had to love me but as a person they did not like me at all. The irony was I never liked them.

There have always been two completely different sides to my family. The public and private. I hated the falseness, the unpredictability. Never knowing what to say in reply to even normal questions about the family.

My mum and dad had been together for a while when they had me. My mum's parents owned a pub, and it just so happened that my dad ended up in a pothole driving past, went into the pub and that is how they met.

They were living in the Middle East when she got pregnant. This was an interesting place at the time. We are talking bombs and chemical weapons leading into the Gulf War in the early nineties. My dad was a surveyor, building hospitals.

My mum came back to the UK to have me. She was alone when she gave birth. There wasn't anyone there to support her.

(In fact, I was also alone when I was giving birth. My mum just dropped me off at the hospital and left me to go in alone. She went and got pissed with the neighbour.)

Once I hit a month old and was able to get all my jabs, we went straight back to the Middle East. I don't remember a great deal from then.

I vaguely remember the house we lived in. I remember the tiled floor and the video machine we had. I remember we lived through USA-enforced sanctions.

When we moved to India, the place we lived in didn't have supermarkets or processed food. It had a small market. There were no shops as such, just people sat on the side of a dusty road with a tarpaulin sheet with their produce on. Cows wandered freely among the traffic and stalls, and added to that were the fishmongers, rotten food, animals. It really was an in-your-face (and nose) experience.

My parents finally split when I was about seventeen years old. We went on a family holiday and right at the beginning, they told us they were getting a divorce. This ruined the whole holiday, and then at the end, they told us that they were actually going to stay together.

I remember my dad saying to me, 'You know it is your fault that we are separating.' My relationship with my dad has always been pretty terrible.

After the separation, he developed this preoccupation with prostitutes. There was my twenty-eighth birthday and we went on holiday, and instead of actually going out to dinner like we had planned, he just hired a prostitute and went out with her. This has happened probably more times than I can count. He always seems to miss my birthdays.

My dad can be detrimental to me. He can be cruel, controlling, manipulative and narcissistic. Emotionally, he was extremely abusive to us all. I was the only one who would answer back and argue. It's fair to say I bore a lot of the brunt.

I had a phone conversation with him just the other day. He has this sense of trying to control and regulate everything, including the conversation. But it was okay. I was able to keep my cool and not react to it and not let it get me upset or frustrated.

## 12th March 2019 – 3:20 a.m.
## Room 221

Liking how resilient I am. Each knockback, I'm bouncing back quicker, better and stronger.

Felt the urge to tidy earlier. I'm not the tidiest at the best of times. As usual with me, what started as a little task led on to another then another. It looks so much better, and I feel so much better.

As I finished up, I thought if I can make this place homely, I can do it anywhere. It's what my mum always did. While ex-pat life may sound glamorous, it isn't always. Fair dues to my mum. Wherever we were, she rolled her sleeves up and made it a home.

She was a real mixed bag. In some ways she was brave. In other ways I felt I was being manipulated. I often felt betrayed by my mum. Whether it was feeling set-up, ridiculed or gossiped about. After the initial hurt, it was the betrayal of it coming from the one person in the world who should have loved me the most.

Betrayal never comes from strangers.

What should be my nearest and dearest, the ones who should protect and support me, the people and agencies that should have built me up, have continuously (apart from the occasional diamond) not only let me down but taken it a step further and fucked me right over.

People say 'You can't save everyone' and 'You can't help those who won't help themselves.' True. The one thing I experienced and worked hard to escape was addiction. It was the elephant in the room with my mum. What most of my extended family don't know is that from ten years old I looked after her when she was drunk, night after night.

My mum was beautiful though. Glowing freckly skin with soft blue eyes and golden blonde hair. She wasn't tall like me. I'd say around 5'3". Never unhealthy thin but slim. She was naturally really attractive. Never wore heavy makeup or looked slaggy.

She was warm and friendly without being flirty. She could talk to anyone. She had a good sense of humour and was well-travelled and interesting. The more I write, the more my writing looks like hers.

I loved my mum so much. I used to cry myself to sleep thinking of losing her. I really thought she would live with me and be there to watch my family grow. Even though there were thirty years between us, I hoped we would die very close together.

I wasn't too bothered about the world. I always just wanted a family to build a future and life with. Live together. Watch my children grow. Have a business we could all work in. We would have enough money to get everything we needed, and we would never be alone because we would always have each other. Family has always been so important to me. I never wanted anything or anyone else.

## 16th March 2019 – 10:50 p.m.
## Room 221

### *Ho-rachy (Ho Hierarchy)*

I find it hard to understand humans. What most take as societal norms rarely make sense to me. I find most of it odd. Marriage, for example. To me, it's basically your dad giving you to another man.

Out of all the confusion that is humanity, females, to me, are the most complex. To me, they are the most tragic, especially the women who seem to drag other women down. It can be a lot more subtle with women. For example, a man cheats on his wife and the wife batters the girlfriend. The bit on the side probably had no idea she was a bit on the side, and now got battered for it. We are expected to support our men, and so often this has the cost of tearing other women down. We need to be supporting each other, not tearing each other down.

So many barbaric things take place under the protection of traditions or culture. Like that covers you. For me, female circumcision highlights this. Those poor little girls. How hard does society have to work to break the female down to the point that an act like that can be seen as a necessary rite of passage?

I believe ancient societies were matriarchal. But there has been a shift to break the female down. Women aren't arm candy—they create life!

I adore my two children, but I feel more protective over Naomi. I feel women have a lot more things associated to them that can take them off-course. Not that it doesn't happen both ways, but I fear my daughter being involved in domestic violence.

Strange thing, domestic violence. So often is it perceived as a choice and having all this stigma around it. There's no such thing as stigma, just shame and even worse, victim shaming.

Sufferers and victims are so often demonised. At a time when you need support and affection, you are pushed away. Made to feel guilty and dirty and that you chose it and that you deserved it. At a time when you have been wronged, others work towards excusing the aggressor and blaming the victim.

One of the saddest sides to humanity.

### 18th March 2019 – 12:20 a.m.
### Room 221

I started drinking and smoking weed at around fourteen. I remember starting to go out clubbing when I was doing my GCSEs around sixteen. We used to just have packs of a hundred pills that we would sell and get these wads of cash. We would run around three nights a week doing this.

I remember the serious drugs starting during a summer vacation with my friends just after my GCSEs. We were staying at this place where there was this pill dealer who lived upstairs. It was there that I met Rhys.

My first job was working in a pub at eighteen years old. I remember really liking it and being able to relate to people well. I remember working in the airport starting in the summer of 2005.

It was around this time I started using heroin. Rhys had a friend who told us you can smoke heroin, and so we did. At this time, we would probably go through about a ten bag every other day. I remember going on a holiday with my mum around this time and that was the first time I really remember getting withdrawals.

I would say probably one of the worst withdrawals was when I was coming off methadone in rehab. I just remember it hurting like hell. I was awake for about seven days just trying to get through it. I remember just having no energy to do anything. I just felt like shit.

At the moment I can spend £25 to £30 daily or every other day on drugs. This amount will last me about an hour. Sometimes I can go two to three days without. I usually use crack.

Sometimes I use heroin; I have snowballs on occasion, which are a mixture of crack and heroin. I would describe crack, the experience of it, as just beautiful. Heroin is a bit weird, but the mix of the two can create something completely different. I can often get mood stabilisers here and there from people. Cannabis or alcohol is there most days, especially if there are other people about.

Spice is around. It is so easily mistaken for weed, and there was a time when I first tried it accidentally. I had three puffs of what I thought was a spliff, but then something wasn't right, and I passed out for who knows how long. It really isn't very good, and I don't like using it frequently. It can be very dangerous, especially if you don't know you are taking it.

I think the most useful pharmaceutical drug I have used was Subutex, which acts on opioid receptors to minimise dependence in a way that I found really beneficial.

I think one big misconception is that I am just getting high all the time and having this great time doing it. It's not really like that. I don't really take drugs to get high; I just take them to feel normal. To be honest, drugs are probably the most consistent and dependable relationship I have had in the past fifteen years.

## 20th March 2019 – 9:35 p.m.
## Room 221

I've never felt like people 'get' me. I think that's why I take it so bad when professionals don't. I'm tired of feeling wrong. I have spent my entire adult life in some sort of treatment.

I moved, attempting to be closer to my family and detox. This didn't really happen. I remember just being on it all the time.

I met Steve three weeks before getting pregnant with my son Aaron. In the beginning he was really nice and supportive. Then he lost his job, and we were spending more and more time together. He was drinking more, and I was smoking. This is when we started arguing. I went into a women's refuge when I was pregnant.

I was twenty-nine when I was pregnant with Aaron. Steve was his dad. I had never really been one for relationships. I was convinced I was going to die a lonely spinster. Yet, here I was with a man who had shown interest in me.

I fell pregnant very early in the relationship, and not only did Steve want to be an active part but he also wanted to stay with me. I was so happy not to be preparing to be a single mum. I loved that we attended every appointment together.

He wanted a boy so bad. I remember holding his hand through the six-month scan. I watched his eyes well up with tears of joy as they told us we were expecting a boy. It was amazing.

I remember the pregnancy being horrible. I was sick so much and I remember having really serious nerve pain and numbness. Having that weight is so hard, especially when you just keep getting bigger and harder and moving just becomes so difficult.

About five weeks after Aaron was born, Steve and I got in a serious argument. He kept holding on to Aaron while we were arguing, and I kept asking him to give him to me or put him somewhere safe. This argument escalated to the point where he was choking me and almost killed me. I went back into refuge.

This is when drug services and social services started to become involved. My experience of social services was one of incompetency and inconsistency. I often felt there were double standards between what was expected of me and what was expected of them. It was like I just constantly had this feeling of being set up to fail.

After Aaron was born, Steve ended up being imprisoned for assault. We weren't together by this point, and he was with another woman. I remember when he went into prison, his new partner was there living in his apartment, and I was homeless with his baby. It was a really difficult time.

I felt that the very people who should have been helping to make my son's life joyful just chipped away at me. I relapsed and had to detox. The first weekend I came back out, the police and social services were at my door. My cousin had rung social services saying I'd been out using all weekend.

After I had Aaron and was separated from Steve, I met Andrew. He was super intelligent. We would just have the best chats and laughs. He had his own difficulties, was open to probation, would drink and struggled with his mental health. He had been in prison at the age of seventeen and could be very abusive.

After we had been together two years, Andrew died. I remember thinking that it was a relief. That same relief I had mentioned previously. I remember not long after, his best mate died as well.

I met my daughter's dad, Darren, in December 2016. Him and Steve had actually shared a cell in prison, what are the fucking odds?

To be honest, the relationship with Darren was a pretty hostile one. I miss him, but it isn't just him I miss, it is his whole family and me being a part of it. His family actually felt like in-laws, you know.

It's like sometimes people are different people with different people, and I liked who I was with them. I seemed to have this thought in the back of my mind that if one day he was able to sort his shit out and I could sort out mine, we might be able to make it work.

We would get on drugs together. I remember a time once I was at home and Darren had gone out. A drug dealer basically broke into our house to collect drugs. I was hiding. I didn't know what to do. I was terrified. This guy was huge and was holding a large knife. I genuinely thought I was going to die that day. I was so scared that I was going to get raped or killed. I was trying to call Darren to warn him that this guy was here, but he had left his phone at home. I could hear it ringing. Darren ended up walking in the front door. The guy stabbed him three times with the knife.

I had called 999 just before it happened. I remember saying 'just run'. I didn't know what else to do. The drug dealer had disappeared, and Darren was taken to hospital. He survived. He told me that I had ruined his life and that he never wanted to see me again.

## 22nd March 2019 – 4:15 a.m.<br>Room 74

Not well at all at the moment. Haven't been good for the past few days. Had the maddest dreams last night.

I was somewhere, like, foreign, and someone had flushed a newborn down the toilet. It turned out there were twins. The healthy-looking tubby one had died, so on a tray they brought something crawling in ants with fruit flies all about it. I had a walkie-talkie and had to repeatedly go through with them what was going on. Kept repeating that one was dead, but there was a survivor. Nobody seemed to do anything, and she was covered in all this blood. Kept thinking of all the bacteria in a toilet. In the end I washed her in the sink where the other baby had been, a tubby, healthy baby, but this second one was like some weird skinny voodoo doll. As I washed her hair, everything kinda disintegrated and where her face was, was just some wire, a bit like a tennis racket. She had really long hair. I panicked, thinking I'd killed her. But whoever it was with me was like, 'Nah, that's fine.' It was like it moved, like when maggots take over. So, I rinsed her hair more and got rid of all that infestation.

Hardly dream anymore. My current partner wished me sweet dreams that night, so he promised not to do that again!

I also keep getting this experience, a memory I guess, of our old house in India. I remember it so vividly; it is like I am there. I can see it all so clearly. I know people are there. I imagine that it is my brother or my mum. I can sense their presence there, but they just aren't there. No matter where I look in the house, I just can't seem to see them.

It's almost five a.m. Feeling slightly better. I feel the best I have for days. I really want some OJ. Gonna get some good fruit juice this week. Tempted to go now.

## 24th March 2019 – 3:20 a.m.
## Room 74

### *My son, Aaron*

I was so excited about becoming a mum, but I couldn't quite let myself enjoy it. My biggest fear had always been losing a child.

I had always wanted children and seen myself as a mum but never quite believed it would happen.

My son is now living with my dad overseas. Currently, he thinks I'm an aunty that lives in the UK. I don't know how this will play out in the future.

I loved watching Aaron sleep.

Children look so peaceful and angelic, and being near them, hearing their little breaths and snores, watching their faces and movements and positions while inhaling those lovely small children smells... that has got to be one of the most relaxing and enjoyable things ever.

I never really felt genuinely connected to anyone until Aaron came along. For three years, we were together all the time.

I remember thinking just how much he impressed me, every day, in small ways. He still does.

As a baby, he was really considerate. When other babies were over or we were out with other kids, he would often go and get toys and bring them back for them. I remember thinking that he is a lot nicer than me.

I remember Aaron being so big he couldn't even fit into those baby seats.

Aaron loves cars. Anything to do with cars, wheels or mechanics, he is just drawn to.

I remember taking him to Folly Farm. He wasn't so interested in the animals, but there was a big tractor there and he did a very good job of inspecting it and making sure it was in good condition.

I remember one day Aaron was doing this really strange action with his arm. It was out straight and with his hand down and he was making this mechanical kind of noise. I didn't really know what he was doing. Then I remembered he loved *Paw Patrol*, and what he was doing was being the crane, lifting and dropping things.

I remember when he was very little, he always had food in both hands. He very much had a sweet tooth. I think he got that from me. He just loved pancakes, especially with Nutella. I remember I would put him in the highchair, take his shirt off and just let him make a mess eating them. He loved it.

He was always so smiley. He has these big brown eyes. He was really sociable. He was really a little man. He had this attitude and swagger about him. Once, I took him to the pub, and he strutted up to these guys who were sitting nearby talking and laughing. He just casually stood by them and when they laughed, he would join in with them as though he was just one of them hanging out.

I remember when he was about seven months old, we lived in Singapore for two months. He just loved it. He had so many photos with the locals. He was like a little celebrity posing for all these photos. He would love getting his photo taken. Sometimes when he was having a tantrum or really upset, he would snap out of it and start posing if I said I would take a photo of him.

I think he has a sense of rebellion and feistiness, which he gets from me. I think he is very clever. He currently knows two languages fluently.

### *My daughter, Naomi*

When Naomi was born, she was seven weeks premature and was less than two kilograms. She soon packed on the weight though and got the name Pudding and Podge because of it.

All I have with Naomi is this image of a baby. But she isn't a tiny baby any longer. She is growing.

I just try and imagine what she looks like. What her hair looks like. What sounds she is making and what words she might be saying. I imagine her eating solid food and I wonder what she likes and what she doesn't like.

I remember when I first held her. I held her for the first week of her life. Come the second week, I could only see her for an hour two days a week.

### 27th March 2019 – 11:55 p.m.
### Room 74

The world can be disappointing and cruel. It can be unfair, uneven and unequal. It can be run by money. The wrong things are often held in high esteem. Things are twisted to justify and cover up other things.

One of the cruellest things I have ever experienced was in 2017 when they took my baby away from me instead of genuinely supporting and helping me. They took Aaron into care. Then they took Naomi away from me. They took both of my babies away from me. My family was destroyed.

There were so many services—social services, family support services, charity organisations, speech pathology, drug services—

and they kept saying 'you've got all this support' but it genuinely felt like none of them was actually trying to help. Just signposting and signposting and collusion.

I felt betrayed. I was scared and fearful. I would just end up withdrawing to try and protect myself and the little I had. I found it harder and harder to cope and harder to work with services who would just keep pressuring me.

I just wanted to be the best I could, but it just kept being unattainable, with moving expectations and double standards. All I ever did was fall apart and ask for help.

My family and my kids are important to me. It is like having your own little safe community that you have created and maintain.

The world can be caring. There is more than enough to go around. Resources such as money, food, housing. No exploitation. Seeing the big picture. Not caught up in superficial products. Actually helping instead of just being 'seen' to help.

I have a beggar friend who goes out on the street and begs daily. Most days when he comes back, he shares everything he received with me and some other people. It is humbling. He knows what it is like to have nothing, and yet he still shares the little he has.

That is what caring is. Wanting to help and offering to others without an agenda and no expectations or owing. It is having nothing, and not only appreciating the little you do have, but sharing it with others. It is about connectedness and being considerate to other people. It is these small, unexpected acts of kindness that show character. It's genuine.

It is like things have a duality to them at the moment. It is and it isn't. There is a sense of karma to it all. It is irony that gets me through. It is pushing the irony. It feels like it is a transition from useless to unusable, especially regarding others.

At the moment, there is a sense of going in the right direction. I seem to be able to just step back. I am carrying on and getting on with it. I am getting stronger and working on self-preservation. I am dealing with things better. There have been glimmers of things not being so flat. Actual excitement. Genuine happiness. Yesterday was a really productive day. I am harder than I thought. Things are happening as they should, in their own fucked-up way.

*Dear Lydia,*

*I think I need to begin by saying thank you. Thank you for sharing your experiences with me. I know it hasn't always been easy to share, and I feel privileged that you have felt comfortable enough to trust me with these experiences.*

*I remember when we first met, we always seemed to be in a small or cluttered room off to the side somewhere in a hostel. I remember you telling me you loved reading and collecting book sets then. I wonder if the Famous Five is something worth revisiting?*

*I remember in those first conversations, you had this idea. You would say, 'I am going to get my own place and get a car and get some furniture to refurnish and up-cycle.' Fast forward to now, and the last time I was at your flat, I walked straight past your car, and just before I left, you showed me the first piece of furniture you had acquired to work on. I hope you feel proud that you have been able to accomplish this.*

*We have had so many conversations about relationships, in all sorts of forms. I remember hearing of your experiences of being homeless and living in hostels, and especially the people that were around. There was a sense of wanting people around for company to cut through that loneliness, but on the other hand, there was this pull into taking responsibility for other people's problems that had nothing to do with you. Perhaps it was that irony you used to mention quite a lot.*

*I have been able to see you intentionally choose who you want present in your life and develop ways of managing the impact that others can have on you. I think you have been able to revise the influence of both people and substances and regain more control over their presence and effect in your life. I hope you can continue to work on this as hard as you have been.*

*I think if there was one recurrent theme that underlined a lot of our conversations, it would have been loss. I remember hearing of the first person you lost, your Grampy. I distinctly remember feeling just how important he was to you and how much you looked up to him.*

*When I first met you, you had not long lost your mum. I remember us discussing the sense of relief. I think this was coupled with stories from childhood of not only attending to, but also feeling responsible for, your mum's drinking and distress. I hope those memories can be held alongside others you shared, ones of remembering her warmth, her beauty and the love you have for her.*

*I remember you saying that you were hesitant to talk about Rhys, but I am thankful you did. I appreciated you telling me of his infectious happiness and hidden creativity. I also remember you telling me of the hurt you felt in losing that half of your soul. Although horrible, I believe that hurt was a testament to just how much you loved him. He will always be there, framed by your window, supporting and encouraging you.*

*I don't pretend to imagine what it was like to have both Aaron and Naomi taken. I do remember you saying that all you have of Naomi is an image of a baby. This stuck with me. I sincerely hope that you are able to keep sending and receiving exchanges with her adopters and that perhaps one day you will be able to meet with her again.*

*There have been numerous times where you have shown me a picture of Aaron. You had the same expression then as when you did when you told me stories about his attitude and swagger. It is the expression of a proud mum. Please cherish every image you have of him for now, and I hope that when the time comes, you will be able to cherish moments with him.*

*Again, thank you. It has been a privilege getting to know you.*

*I wish you all the best for the future.*

*Please take care of yourself.*

*Warmly,*

*Lewis*

# 32 Lessons Learnt in Life

*Enfys Roberts*

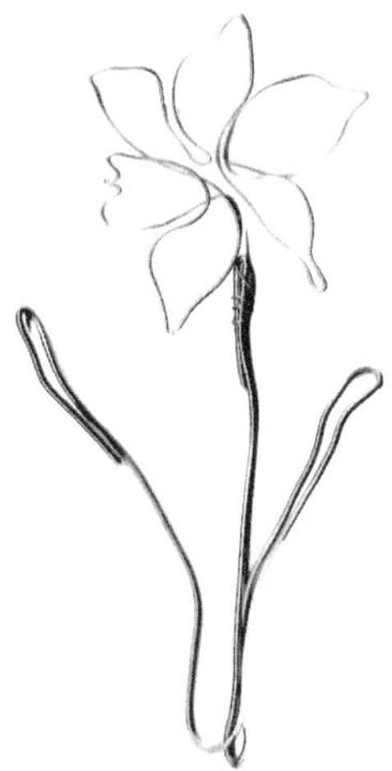


59

## *Lessons from Childhood and School*

I was born in June 1989.

My parents were still technically together, but they weren't really. My dad was having affairs left, right and centre when my mum was pregnant with me.

We lived in a flat, just on the corner next to the house I live in now. There was me, my mum and my brother, Andrew. My dad was around a bit, but not much. When I was about a year and a half, we moved house.

Apparently, when I was eight weeks old, my dad threw me across a twelve-foot room. My mum then punched him across the room. When I was two years old, my mum was cooking and holding me at the same time, and I got burnt on the face by the oven door.

**Lesson #1:**
**Parents may not be the best at looking after you.**

I went to my first primary school from nursery to year three. I got excluded for punching a teacher. I remember Mum being called. She came and picked me up from school and took me for a cuppa.

**Lesson #2:**
**If you punch a teacher, you get to leave school and have tea with your mum.**

I then went to a different primary from year four to year six. I remember one time not being allowed to go to the toilet, so I just peed on my chair. They had to phone my mum to bring a change of clothes.

I went to my first high school from year seven to the start of year nine. At the beginning of year nine, I stabbed a learning support teacher with scissors. I got expelled.

**Lesson #3:**
**Best not to stab teachers with scissors.**

I then went to a farm school just outside of town. We had standard classes in the morning—math, English, etc.—and then in the afternoon, we had farm-based activities such as pottery, music etc. I always did horse riding. I was the only one brave enough to actually ride a horse.

I remember I used to go nuts sometimes when I was at the farm. I would hit teachers, and then they would have to restrain me.

**Lesson #4:**
**Don't be a little shit in school.**

For years ten and eleven, I went to a comprehensive school to do my GCSEs. This school doesn't even exist anymore. I didn't really act up at this school. I think it had something to do with my foster parents and being in foster care.

Then, when I finished my GCSEs, I went into college. I completed Level One and Two NVQ in Hospitality and Cookery and Level Two in Food and Drink Service. But I never want to do hospitality again. In fact, I burn toast if I try and make it.

**Lesson #5:**
**Hospitality sucks! (In other words, hospitality and cooking in general is not for me.)**

When I was five years old, I met my brother, sister and Nan for the first time. My brother and sister are both much older than me (by about nineteen years).

**Lesson #6:**
**Your family may be bigger than you think.**

When I was six years old, I was in a car crash. I was actually in a minibus with fifteen other people. I remember getting knocked off my chair and getting a cut along my head.

**Lesson #7:**
**Buses are unsafe.**

When I was little, my brother Andrew used to pinch my mum's money and blame it on me. Then he would say he knew where it was and go get it for her as though he was the innocent one.

**Lesson #8:**
**Siblings can't be trusted.**

I remember when I was about nine years old, my mum washed my mouth out with soap for saying "Fuck off, you cunt." The soap was disgusting. I still swear now though.

**Lesson #9:**
**Soap in your mouth is gross and does not stop people swearing.**

When I was about ten years old, I had thirteen teeth out because they were rotten. As an adult now, I have a lot of rotten teeth and the dentist is in the process of taking them all out.

**Lesson #10:**
**You should probably look after your teeth.**

I started drinking and using cannabis when I was about twelve.

I remember being arrested a few times around twelve years old. That was primarily for hitting my mum and threatening to stab her. Often, I was the one who called the police.

**Lesson #11:**
**Best not to get drunk and stoned at twelve years old, threaten to stab your mum, then call the police.**

I remember running away from home often. I ran up to the school farm once. My mum was quite old, and I remember I used to tell other kids that she was my Nan and that my real mum was in prison for drugs.

**Lesson #12:**
**At thirteen years old, street cred is important.**

I went into care when I was thirteen. My foster parents were Lily and Oli. The children were Jack, Charlie, Olivia, Sophie, Grace, Ava, Rachel, Elly and me. Some of us got along; some of us didn't. I stayed there for two and a half years.

It was different and strict living in foster care. My foster parents would listen, and they would have rules but still let you do your own thing. I remember the first night I was there I was supposed to be back at nine p.m. but I got back at eleven. I had been out with Sophie, and she broke my watch. She slept out, but I went back.

We used to have to clean the whole house once a week. We would get £7 pocket money. I usually used it to go see my mum.

**Lesson #13:**
**If you have a good foster family, things can be strict, but you can still have some freedom. Chances are you may not all get along.**

At fifteen I left care and returned to my mum. From the ages of sixteen to eighteen, I was in college. My mum had a stroke three days before my eighteenth birthday.

From the ages of eighteen to twenty-one, I was my mum's full-time carer. She couldn't speak after the stroke. I think we would both get really frustrated at each other when we couldn't communicate. I would often just walk out. I used to cook and give her tablets and constantly check on her to make sure she was okay.

I remember when she re-learnt to speak; one of the first things she said was "fuck off." I remember laughing so hard the first time she said it, and then she was trying to tell me to stop laughing but all she could say was "fuck off." My relationship with my mum has been pretty funny. We get on really well.

**Lesson #14:**
**It is (inappropriately) funny if swearing is your only way to communicate.**

### *Lessons about Relationships*

I started getting into relationships in my twenties. I have been in four relationships which have become really violent.

**Lesson #15:**
**Don't get in or continue to be in violent relationships.**

At twenty, I got married. His name was Ahraz and he was a practising Muslim. We met through an online dating app. I remember he used to say things like "You are the light to my darkness" and "I have never seen an angel like you before." We were together for about four weeks, and then we got married.

**Lesson #16:**
**It might be best not to get married after four weeks of being together.**

The marriage was in a mosque, and my aunty and uncle came to witness. I remember the day after we were married, I went across the road to the shop and bought some bacon to cook up for breakfast.

I didn't know I wasn't supposed to eat it now. How was I supposed to know? You should have seen his face. If looks could kill, I would have been dead fifty times over.

**Lesson #17:**
**Learn what the religion is about before marrying someone religious.**

So, we ended up splitting up after four weeks of marriage. The whole relationship only really lasted two months. I'd got into another relationship, and he was cheating on me anyways. We never even really consummated the marriage once it happened. I was meant to get a dowry of £1000. I sent a couple of mates to go and try to get it. They ended up in prison. I still never got that money.

**Lesson #18:**
**You never get your dowry, even if you send badass guys to go get it.**

I then moved in with Darren. There was lots of drinking. It wasn't good. He was actually one of my mate's dads. It goes to say he was a bit older than me. I was about twenty; he was fifty-two at the time. Some of his kids were older than me. I lived with him and his sixteen-year-old son. I was there for about two months. It was somewhere to live.

**Lesson #19:**
**Me + Darren + alcohol = not so good.**

I remember one day I went out, got pissed and was hanging out with this guy, kissing him. I went back home but had decided to go back out and stay at a mate's house for the night. Darren and I got in an argument over this and the fact that I was kissing this other guy. It ended up with him having me pinned up against the wall with a knife to my throat. I just laughed in his face, saying "You think that will stop me?"

**Lesson #20:**
**Don't get pinned up against a wall with a knife to your throat.**

So, the police arrived; most likely a neighbour had called them. They said I had to leave, so I ended up at my mate's house. I still ended up staying with Darren for another couple of months. Eventually, it got too much, and I said I needed to stay with a friend to help babysit, and I just never went back. He is with my cousin now.

**Lesson #21:**
**If a relationship isn't working, leave.**

Now that I think about it, a lot of the men that have been closely involved in my life are imprisoned. My dad has been in and out; most recently he is in court for paedophilia. My brother was supposed to go to court for racially motivated assault, but he never turned up for court. He is on the run at the moment. I have an uncle in prison as well, and numerous male friends.

**Lesson #22:**
**A lot of men I know go to prison...or should be there.**

I remember when I was pregnant, neither of the kids' dads were around. Rhys' dad was probably out somewhere shagging other people. Social services deemed that Paige's dad wasn't allowed to be around due to the risk he posed.

**Lesson #23:**
**Some men just can't be trusted or relied upon.**

## *Lessons from Adulthood*

One of the first things people notice about me is that I have lots of tattoos. At the moment I have about forty-six. I have my two kids' faces, names and dates of birth. I have my grandparents' and great grandparents' names, dates of birth and the dates they passed. I have my nieces' and nephews' names. I have my sister's and mum's names and dates of birth. I have six ex's names. I have two separate flowers, two animals and a fairy. I also have eight finger tattoos. I have a lot of quotes as well, which I guess are lessons.

**Lesson #24:**
**"Never say goodbye because goodbye means going away and going away means forgetting."**

**Lesson #25:**
**"Learn from yesterday, live for today, hope for tomorrow."**

I was a tattoo artist for a whole week. I did a total of four tattoos. I remember I did one plain love heart and another love heart with "Mum" written in it, and some initials.

**Lesson #26:**
**I am not a tattoo artist.**

## *Lessons from Pregnancy*

I remember when I was pregnant with Rhys, I would crave peanut butter. I had a friend who was making a cooked dinner, and all I could smell was peanut butter. I asked her why she was cooking peanut butter, and she replied, "I'm not; it's just your cravings". I used to really crave chicken mayo baguettes from Greggs. I don't think I was really supposed to be eating those, as you are not supposed to have homemade mayo when you're pregnant. I remember with Paige I craved spaghetti bolognese and Polo mints.

**Lesson #27:**
**Your senses can do strange things when you are pregnant.**

I found it weird being pregnant. I didn't really believe that I was pregnant, even after the scans. I didn't even feel Rhys move at all during the pregnancy. I remember the first time I felt Paige move, I shat myself it was so weird. Not literally.

I remember when I was pregnant and there was a group of family and friends chatting out the front of the house. I came running out of the house. I must have been in a hurry for something. I ended up running straight into a girl from up the street and went arse over tit on the bonnet of a parked car.

**Lesson #28:**
**Don't run while pregnant.**

Lesson #28 reminds me of another story, not related to pregnancy. When I was seventeen and I got really rat-arsed drunk. I was running down the street, fell and went flying. I then went face-first into the pavement.

**Lesson #29:**
**Don't run while drunk.**

Also, when I was twenty-six, I went to the shops and was rushing to get home, so I ran out. I then fell on the curb and broke my ankle.

**Lesson #30:**
**Breaking your ankle hurts.**

**Lesson #31:**
**Just don't run.**

I remember when I was in the hospital going through labour with Paige. They had given me a spinal block so that they could put a stitch in my cervix to stop the labour. I was left on my own and I was sure I needed to pee. So, I tried to stand up. I fell flat on the floor, bum first. I had to wait there for forty-five minutes as I couldn't reach the nurse button for assistance.

**Lesson #32:**
**If you get a spinal block, don't try to walk.**

# Matters of the Heart

*Enfys Roberts*

69

My son Rhys was born in July 2014.
He was twelve weeks early.
He was one pound, twelve ounces.

My daughter Paige was born in June 2016.
She was ten weeks early.
She was three pounds, seven ounces.

**I love and miss my kids.**

My heart feels...
I don't know.
Shit.
Broken.
Crushed.
Ripped out.
Sad.
Like a big black hole.

Rhys and Paige were taken from me in June 2018.
Not long before their birthdays.
That was the day my heart got ripped out.
I was at home.
The kids were home.
I had just got back from court.

The court decided the children would be taken into care.
I had some alcohol on the way back.
Social services turned up and took the children to a friend's house.
I was left there on my own.

It felt so horrible.
I was alone.
I was full of sorrow.

I just drank more alcohol.
I probably drank fourteen to fifteen cans of cider.
I wanted to drown my sorrow.

**I love and miss my kids.**

I would like my heart to feel fixed.
Not as bad as it is now.
I would like it to feel happy, full.
Like nothing could break it.

I remember a day when my heart felt full.
It was the day before they were removed.
We went to the water park.
There was me and my friend Claire with my kids and hers.
We had a picnic and watched the kids play.
They would play on the swings and go on the slide.
I would just enjoy watching them.

It felt lush.
It felt amazing.
I felt happy.

I just watched them play.
I just wanted to keep watching them play.

**I love and miss my kids.**

At the minute it is like all my happiness,
joy and love are being sucked into a big black hole.

I hold onto the love that will always be there for my children.
That love will never go away.

There are times when I don't think about them.
When I am distracted.
I then feel really guilty for being distracted and think that it is not okay.

Sometimes it is okay to think about other things and look after myself.
I want to try and go for walks on the beach.
I find it calm and relaxing.
I have just started reading.
I got through four chapters of a book yesterday, which is new for me.

**But really, I think about them all the time.**

Every day, I think about them.
Often, I get depressed.
I feel guilty.
I get upset that I will not see them grow up.
I try and think of the things they are doing.
That makes me feel better.
Feel okay.
I imagine them on day trips and doing things I couldn't do with them.
I remind myself that they are okay and are doing well.

I often wonder if they are thinking about me.

If Rhys was here and we asked him, "What is the best thing about your mum?"
He would probably say...

"You are the best mum in the world."
"You take me to the park and let me go on YouTube."

If Paige was here and we asked her, "What is the best thing about your mum?"
She would probably say...
"She gives the BEST cuddles."

**I love my kids.
I really miss them.**

*Dear Enfys,*

*We have been through quite a lot, haven't we? I think the first hurdle we were able to get over was having to get £9000 off your electric and gas meter that was never supposed to be there. What an ordeal that was! I am not sure how many phone calls we made to that company. But the debt got removed and you were able to change supplier.*

*Since then, you have continued to work on numerous aspects of your life. You have managed to get your finances more stable as well as work towards thirty-eight weeks of abstinence. Even with lots of things going on, including an eviction and a lapse, you independently sought out support and have maintained your abstinence.*

*Throughout our time working together I have witnessed numerous difficulties you have had with housing. I can only imagine the sorrow and loneliness that you must have felt continuing to live in such a big house on your own, with the memories of your children in every room. I understand, especially when I first met you, why you would always have the house filled with people staying to keep you company.*

*Unfortunately, some of this company wasn't the best, which resulted in you getting arrested, a few police visits and eventually an eviction. During this time, and still now, I am amazed by your resourcefulness in finding support and safe places to stay.*

*I don't think I could get through this letter without mentioning our trips to the hospital dentist department. I remember once we were in a hurry to get there, and you enquired whether we had enough time for you to 'pop in and get your eyebrows done' first. There is one word that comes to mind when I think of these appointments and that is: brave. Despite the difficulties and instability you were experiencing day to day, you were able to commit to seeing the dentist. To have eight appointments with over fifteen teeth removed, with who knows how many antiseptic needles and stitches. This is the definition of brave.*

*I think the thing I will remember most about our work together is our countless conversations, be that in the car, in a waiting room, in a lounge, walking along the seaside, or just sitting there having a hot chocolate, looking at the ocean. It has been a privilege to hear your stories of growing up and the things you have experienced. You have a gift to be able to tell stories that are personal, to the point, and also comical and relatable. I am so glad we have been able to document and share some of these stories.*

*Within these conversations we have been able to talk a lot about Rhys and Paige. We have been able to talk through the difficulties you were experiencing while they were under your care, as well as the ongoing heartbreak and sorrow since they have been removed. Throughout these conversations, what was most apparent was just how much you love and miss your children, and how not a day goes by where you don't think about them and hold them close in your heart.*

*Finally, I would just like to say thank you. I have learnt a lot from you. Not just where the best doughnuts are, but how to persevere and laugh, even when things seem hopeless.*

*I hope that in the future you are able to find comfort, support and love among family and friends. I hope that your confidence in yourself continues to grow, and I hope you continue to contribute to those around you because you have a lot to offer. Please take the time to cherish moments of joy, no matter how small and few.*

*I wish you all the best for the future.*

*Please take care.*

*Warmly,*

*Lewis*

# References

Broadhurst, K. & Mason, C. (2013). Maternal outcasts: Raising the profile of women who are vulnerable to successive, compulsory removals of their children – a plea for preventative action, *Journal of Social Welfare and Family Law*, 35(3), 291–304, DOI: 10.1080/09649069.2013.805061

Broadhurst, K. & Mason, C. (2017). Birth parents and the collateral consequences of court-ordered child removal: Towards a comprehensive framework. *International Journal of Law, Policy and the Family*, 31(1), 41–59. https://doi.org/10.1093/lawfam/ebw013

Broadhurst, K., Mason, C., Bedston, S., Alrouh, B., Morriss, L., McQuarrie, T., Palmer, M., Shaw, M., Harwin, J. & Kershaw, S. (2017). *Vulnerable Birth Mothers and Recurrent Care Proceedings. Final Main Report.* Retrieved from: http://wp.lancs.ac.uk/recurrent-care/publications/

Bruner, J. (1986). *Actual Minds, Possible Worlds.* Cambridge, MA: Harvard University Press.

Bruner, J. (1990). *Acts of meaning.* Cambridge, MA: Harvard University Press.

Denborough, D. (2008). *Collective Narrative Practice: Responding to Individuals, Groups, and Communities who Have Experienced Trauma.* Adelaide, Australia: Dulwich Centre Publications.

Doka, K. (1989). *Disenfranchised grief: Recognizing hidden sorrow.* Lexington, MA: Lexington Books.

Doka, K. (2017). Disenfranchised grief and trauma. In N. Thompson, G. Cox & R. Stevenson (Ed.), *Handbook of Traumatic Loss: A Guide to Theory and Practice* (pp. 377–387). Abingdon, UK: Routledge.

Epston, D. & White, M. (1992). *Experience, contradiction, narrative & imagination.* Adelaide: Dulwich Centre Publications.

Gaddis, S. (2016). Poststructural Inquiry: Narrative Therapy's De-Centered and Influential Stance. In *Poststructural and Narrative Thinking in Family Therapy* (pp. 9–27). Springer International Publishing.

Hughes, D. (1997). *What can a counsellor do? A personal account of counselling by a mother who parted with her child for adoption.* London, UK: Post Adoption Centre.

Memarnia, N., Nolte, L., Norris, C. & Harborne, A. (2015). 'It felt like it was night all the time': listening to the experiences of birth mothers whose children have been taken into care or adopted. *Adoption and Fostering,* 39(4): 303–317. https://doi.org/10.1177/0308575915611516

Myerhoff, B. (1982). Life history among the elderly: Performance, visibility and remembering. In J. Ruby (Ed.), *A crack in the mirror: Reflexive perspective in anthropology* (pp. 99–117). Philadelphia: University of Pennsylvania Press.

Neil, E. (2017). *Helping birth parents in adoption. A literature review of birth parent support services, including supporting post adoption contact. An expertise for the German Research Center on Adoption (EFZA).* Deutsches Jugendinstitut. Retrieved from: https://pdfs.semanticscholar.org/d89d/e180202bf0f0e11395ba73efb90fd3ba9731.pdf.

Pupavac, V. (2001). Therapeutic governance: Psycho-social intervention and trauma risk management. *Disasters,* 25(4), 358–372. https://doi.org/10.1111/1467-7717.00184

Rober, P. & Seltzer, M. (2010). Avoiding colonizer positions in the therapy room: Some ideas about the challenges of dealing with the dialectic of misery and resources in families. *Family process,* 49(1), 123–137. DOI: 10.1111/j.1545-5300.2010.01312.x

Roberts, L., Meakings, S., Forrester, D., Smith, A. and Shelton, K. (2017). Care-leavers and their children placed for adoption. *Children and Youth Services Review,* 79, 355–361. https://doi.org/10.1016/j.childyouth.2017.06.030

Roberts, L., Maxwell, N., Messenger, R. & Palmer, C. (2018). Evaluation of reflect in Gwent: Final report. Retrieved from http://orca.cf.ac.uk/123258/

Robinson, E. (2002). Post-adoption grief counselling. *Adoption and Fostering,* 26(2), 57–63. https://doi.org/10.1177/030857590202600208

Robinson, R. (2007). Long term outcomes of losing a child through adoption: The impact of disenfranchised grief. *Grief Matters,* 10(1), pp. 8–11. Retrieved from: https://search.informit.com.au/documentSummary;dn=056445937745243;res=IELFSC ISSN: 1440-6888

Schauer, M., Neuner, F. & Elbert, T. (2011). *Narrative exposure therapy: A short-term treatment for traumatic stress disorders.* Cambridge, MA: Hogrefe Publishing.

Waters, T. E. A. & Fivush, R. (2015). Relations between narrative coherence, identity, and psychological well-being in emerging adulthood. *J. Pers.* 83, 441–451. DOI: 10.1111/jopy.12120

White, M. (1988). Saying hullo again: The incorporation of the lost relationship in the resolution of grief. In C. White & D. Denborough (Ch 2.) *Introducing Narrative Therapy: A collection of practice-based writings* (pp. 17–29). Adelaide, Australia: Dulwich Centre Publications.

White, M. (2005). *Workshop notes.* Retrieved from: http://www.dulwichcentre.com.au/michael-white-workshop-notes.pdf. Retrieved 30 August 2017.

White, M. (2007). *Maps of narrative practice.* New York, NY: WW Norton.

## Publisher Information

Rowanvale Books provides publishing services to independent authors, writers and poets all over the globe. We deliver a personal, honest and efficient service that allows authors to see their work published, while remaining in control of the process and retaining their creativity. By making publishing services available to authors in a cost-effective and ethical way, we at Rowanvale Books hope to ensure that the local, national and international community benefits from a steady stream of good quality literature.

For more information about us, our authors or our publications, please get in touch.

www.rowanvalebooks.com
info@rowanvalebooks.com

www.ingramcontent.com/pod-product-compliance
Ingram Content Group UK Ltd.
Pitfield, Milton Keynes, MK11 3LW, UK
UKHW041644190726
13854UKWH00006B/2685

9 781914 422164